2021

JANUARY

S	M	T	W	T	F	S
					1	2
3	4	5	6	7	8	9
10	11	12	13	14	15	16
17	18	19	20	21	22	23
24	25	26	27	28	29	30
31						

FEBRUARY

S	M	T	W	T	F	S
	1	2	3	4	5	6
7	8	9	10	11	12	13
14	15	16	17	18	19	20
21	22	23	24	25	26	27
28						

MARCH

S	M	T	W	T	F	S
	1	2	3	4	5	6
7	8	9	10	11	12	13
14	15	16	17	18	19	20
21	22	23	24	25	26	27
28	29	30	31			

APRIL

S	M	T	W	T	F	S
				1	2	3
4	5	6	7	8	9	10
11	12	13	14	15	16	17
18	19	20	21	22	23	24
25	26	27	28	29	30	

MAY

S	M	T	W	T	F	S
						1
2	3	4	5	6	7	8
9	10	11	12	13	14	15
16	17	18	19	20	21	22
23	24	25	26	27	28	29
30	31					

JUNE

S	M	T	W	T	F	S
		1	2	3	4	5
6	7	8	9	10	11	12
13	14	15	16	17	18	19
20	21	22	23	24	25	26
27	28	29	30			

JULY

S	M	T	W	T	F	S
				1	2	3
4	5	6	7	8	9	10
11	12	13	14	15	16	17
18	19	20	21	22	23	24
25	26	27	28	29	30	31

AUGUST

S	M	T	W	T	F	S
1	2	3	4	5	6	7
8	9	10	11	12	13	14
15	16	17	18	19	20	21
22	23	24	25	26	27	28
29	30	31				

SEPTEMBER

S	M	T	W	T	F	S
			1	2	3	4
5	6	7	8	9	10	11
12	13	14	15	16	17	18
19	20	21	22	23	24	25
26	27	28	29	30		

OCTOBER

S	M	T	W	T	F	S
					1	2
3	4	5	6	7	8	9
10	11	12	13	14	15	16
17	18	19	20	21	22	23
24	25	26	27	28	29	30
31						

NOVEMBER

S	M	T	W	T	F	S
	1	2	3	4	5	6
7	8	9	10	11	12	13
14	15	16	17	18	19	20
21	22	23	24	25	26	27
28	29	30				

DECEMBER

S	M	T	W	T	F	S
			1	2	3	4
5	6	7	8	9	10	11
12	13	14	15	16	17	18
19	20	21	22	23	24	25
26	27	28	29	30	31	

JANUARY

SUNDAY	MONDAY	TUESDAY
3	4	5
10	11	12
17	18	19
24	25 Martin Luther King. Jr. Day	26
31		

2021

WEDNESDAY	THURSDAY	FRIDAY	SATURDAY
		1 New Year's Day	2
6	7	8	9
13	14	15	16
20	21	22	23
27	28	29	30

FEBRUARY

SUNDAY	MONDAY	TUESDAY
	1	2
7	8	9
14 Valentine's Day	15 Presidents' Day	16
21	22	23
28		

2021

WEDNESDAY	THURSDAY	FRIDAY	SATURDAY
3	4	5	6
10	11	12	13
17	18	19	20
24	25	26	27

MARCH

SUNDAY	MONDAY	TUESDAY
	1	2
7	8	9
14 Daylight Savings Time Begins	15	16
21	22	23
28 Passover Begins	29	30

2021

WEDNESDAY	THURSDAY	FRIDAY	SATURDAY
3	4	5	6
10	11	12	13
17 St. Patrick's Day	18	19	20 First Day of Spring
24	25	26	27
31			

APRIL

NOTES

SUNDAY	MONDAY	TUESDAY
4 Easter	5	6
11	12	13
18	19	20
25	26	27

2021

WEDNESDAY	THURSDAY	FRIDAY	SATURDAY
	1 April Fool's Day	2	3
7	8	9	10
14	15	16	17
21	22	23	24
28	29	30	

MAY

NOTES

SUNDAY	MONDAY	TUESDAY
2	3	4
9 Mother's Day	10	11
16	17	18
23 30	24 Memorial Day 31	25

2021

WEDNESDAY	THURSDAY	FRIDAY	SATURDAY
			1
5	6	7	8
12	13	14	15
19	20	21	22
26	27	28	29

JUNE

NOTES

SUNDAY	MONDAY	TUESDAY
		1
6	7	8
13	14	15
20 Father's Day First Day of Summer	21	22
27	28	29

2021

WEDNESDAY	THURSDAY	FRIDAY	SATURDAY
2	3	4	5
9	10	11	12
16	17	18	19
23	24	25	26
30			

JULY

SUNDAY	MONDAY	TUESDAY
4 Independence Day	5	6
11	12	13
18	19	20
25	26	27

2021

WEDNESDAY	THURSDAY	FRIDAY	SATURDAY
	1	2	3
7	8	9	10
14	15	16	17
21	22	23	24
28	29	30	31

AUGUST

SUNDAY	MONDAY	TUESDAY
1	2	3
8	9	10
15	16	17
22	23	24
29	30	31

2021

WEDNESDAY	THURSDAY	FRIDAY	SATURDAY
4	5	6	7
11	12	13	14
18	19	20	21
25	26	27	28

SEPTEMBER

NOTES

SUNDAY	MONDAY	TUESDAY
5	6	7
	Labor Day	
12	13	14
19	20	21
26	27	28

2021

WEDNESDAY	THURSDAY	FRIDAY	SATURDAY
1	2	3	4
8	9	10	11 Patriot Day
15	16	17	18
22 First Day of Autumn	23	24	25
29	30		

OCTOBER

SUNDAY	MONDAY	TUESDAY
3	4	5
10	11	12
	Columbus Day	
17	18	19
24	25	26
Halloween 31		

2021

WEDNESDAY	THURSDAY	FRIDAY	SATURDAY
		1	2
6	7	8	9
13	14	15	16
20	21	22	23
27	28	29	30

NOVEMBER

NOTES

SUNDAY	MONDAY	TUESDAY
	1	2
7 Daylight Saving Time Ends	8	9
14	15	16
21	22	23
28 Hanukkah Begins	29	30

2021

WEDNESDAY	THURSDAY	FRIDAY	SATURDAY
3	4	5	6
10	11 Veterans Day	12	13
17	18	19	20
24	25 Thanksgiving	26	27

DECEMBER

NOTES

SUNDAY	MONDAY	TUESDAY
5	6	7
12	13	14
19	20	21
		First Day of Winter
26	27	28

2021

WEDNESDAY	THURSDAY	FRIDAY	SATURDAY
1	2	3	4
8	9	10	11
15	16	17	18
22	23	24 Christmas Eve	25 Christmas
29	30	31 New Year's Eve	

DECEMBER

S M T W T F S
1 2 3 4 5
6 7 8 9 10 11 12
13 14 15 16 17 18 19
20 21 22 23 24 25 26
27 28 29 30 31

28 MONDAY

29 TUESDAY

30 WEDNESDAY

31 THURSDAY

JANUARY

1 FRIDAY

2 SATURDAY

3 SUNDAY

HABIT TRACKER	M	T	W	T	F	S	S

Write a poem.

JANUARY

4   MONDAY

5   TUESDAY

6   WEDNESDAY

7   THURSDAY

8 FRIDAY

9 SATURDAY

10 SUNDAY

HABIT TRACKER	M	T	W	T	F	S	S

Do what makes your heart sing.

JANUARY

11 MONDAY

12 TUESDAY

13 WEDNESDAY

14 THURSDAY

15 FRIDAY

16 SATURDAY

17 SUNDAY

HABIT TRACKER	M	T	W	T	F	S	S

Who is your favorite person?

JANUARY

18 MONDAY

19 TUESDAY

20 WEDNESDAY

21 THURSDAY

22 FRIDAY

23 SATURDAY

24 SUNDAY

HABIT TRACKER	M	T	W	T	F	S	S

Imagine your perfect life.

JANUARY

25 MONDAY

26 TUESDAY

27 WEDNESDAY

28 THURSDAY

29 FRIDAY

30 SATURDAY

31 SUNDAY

HABIT TRACKER	M	T	W	T	F	S	S

Take a walk in nature.

FEBRUARY

1 MONDAY

2 TUESDAY

3 WEDNESDAY

4 THURSDAY

5 FRIDAY

6 SATURDAY

7 SUNDAY

HABIT TRACKER	M	T	W	T	F	S	S

What are you thankful for?

FEBRUARY

8 MONDAY

9 TUESDAY

10 WEDNESDAY

11 THURSDAY

12 FRIDAY

13 SATURDAY

14 SUNDAY

HABIT TRACKER	M	T	W	T	F	S	S

Do it for you.

FEBRUARY

15 MONDAY

16 TUESDAY

17 WEDNESDAY

18 THURSDAY

19 FRIDAY

20 SATURDAY

21 SUNDAY

HABIT TRACKER	M	T	W	T	F	S	S

Who have you helped?

FEBRUARY

22 MONDAY

23 TUESDAY

24 WEDNESDAY

25 THURSDAY

26 FRIDAY

27 SATURDAY

28 SUNDAY

HABIT TRACKER	M	T	W	T	F	S	S

What are your strengths?

MARCH

1	MONDAY

2	TUESDAY

3	WEDNESDAY

4	THURSDAY

S	M	T	W	T	F	S
		1	2	3	4	5	6
7	8	9	10	11	12	13
14	15	16	17	18	19	20
21	22	23	24	25	26	27
28	29	30	31			

5 FRIDAY

6 SATURDAY

7 SUNDAY

HABIT TRACKER	M	T	W	T	F	S	S

What would make your inner child happy?

MARCH

8 MONDAY

9 TUESDAY

10 WEDNESDAY

11 THURSDAY

S	M	T	W	T	F	S
		1	2	3	4	5	6
7	8	9	10	11	12	13
14	15	16	17	18	19	20
21	22	23	24	25	26	27
28	29	30	31			

12 FRIDAY

13 SATURDAY

14 SUNDAY

HABIT TRACKER	M	T	W	T	F	S	S

Love yourself.

MARCH

15 MONDAY

16 TUESDAY

17 WEDNESDAY

18 THURSDAY

S	M	T	W	T	F	S
		1	2	3	4	5	6
7	8	9	10	11	12	13
14	15	16	17	18	19	20
21	22	23	24	25	26	27
28	29	30	31			

19 FRIDAY

20 SATURDAY

21 SUNDAY

HABIT TRACKER	M	T	W	T	F	S	S

Make a plan.

MARCH

22 MONDAY

23 TUESDAY

24 WEDNESDAY

25 THURSDAY

S	M	T	W	T	F	S
		1	2	3	4	5	6
7	8	9	10	11	12	13
14	15	16	17	18	19	20
21	22	23	24	25	26	27
28	29	30	31			

26 FRIDAY

27 SATURDAY

28 SUNDAY

HABIT TRACKER	M	T	W	T	F	S	S

Daydream.

MARCH

S	M	T	W	T	F	S
		1	2	3	4	5	6
7	8	9	10	11	12	13
14	15	16	17	18	19	20
21	22	23	24	25	26	27
28	29	30	31			

29 MONDAY

30 TUESDAY

31 WEDNESDAY

1 THURSDAY

APRIL

S	M	T	W	T	F	S
				1	2	3
4	5	6	7	8	9	10
11	12	13	14	15	16	17
18	19	20	21	22	23	24
25	26	27	28	29	30	

2 FRIDAY

3 SATURDAY

4 SUNDAY

HABIT TRACKER	M	T	W	T	F	S	S

Follow your heart.

APRIL

5   MONDAY

6   TUESDAY

7   WEDNESDAY

8   THURSDAY

S	M	T	W	T	F	S
					1	2	3
4	5	6	7	8	9	10
11	12	13	14	15	16	17
18	19	20	21	22	23	24
25	26	27	28	29	30	

9 FRIDAY

10 SATURDAY

11 SUNDAY

HABIT TRACKER	M	T	W	T	F	S	S

Breathe.

APRIL

12 MONDAY

13 TUESDAY

14 WEDNESDAY

15 THURSDAY

S	M	T	W	T	F	S
				1	2	3
4	5	6	7	8	9	10
11	12	13	14	15	16	17
18	19	20	21	22	23	24
25	26	27	28	29	30	

16 FRIDAY

17 SATURDAY

18 SUNDAY

HABIT TRACKER	M	T	W	T	F	S	S

What does your perfect day look like?

APRIL

19 MONDAY

20 TUESDAY

21 WEDNESDAY

22 THURSDAY

S	M	T	W	T	F	S
				1	2	3
4	5	6	7	8	9	10
11	12	13	14	15	16	17
18	19	20	21	22	23	24
25	26	27	28	29	30	

23 FRIDAY

24 SATURDAY

25 SUNDAY

HABIT TRACKER	M	T	W	T	F	S	S

What lights you up?

APRIL

S M T W T F S
1 2 3
4 5 6 7 8 9 10
11 12 13 14 15 16 17
18 19 20 21 22 23 24
25 26 27 28 29 30

26 MONDAY

27 TUESDAY

28 WEDNESDAY

29 THURSDAY

MAY

S	M	T	W	T	F	S
						1
2	3	4	5	6	7	8
9	10	11	12	13	14	15
16	17	18	19	20	21	22
23	24	25	26	27	28	29
30	31					

30 FRIDAY

1 SATURDAY

2 SUNDAY

HABIT TRACKER	M	T	W	T	F	S	S

Listen to your favorite music.

MAY

3 MONDAY

4 TUESDAY

5 WEDNESDAY

6 THURSDAY

S	M	T	W	T	F	S
						1
2	3	4	5	6	7	8
9	10	11	12	13	14	15
16	17	18	19	20	21	22
23	24	25	26	27	28	29
30	31					

7 FRIDAY

8 SATURDAY

9 SUNDAY

HABIT TRACKER	M	T	W	T	F	S	S

What are your three life goals?

MAY

10 MONDAY

11 TUESDAY

12 WEDNESDAY

13 THURSDAY

S	M	T	W	T	F	S
						1
2	3	4	5	6	7	8
9	10	11	12	13	14	15
16	17	18	19	20	21	22
23	24	25	26	27	28	29
30	31					

14 FRIDAY

15 SATURDAY

16 SUNDAY

HABIT TRACKER	M	T	W	T	F	S	S

How can you be kind to yourself?

MAY

17 MONDAY

18 TUESDAY

19 WEDNESDAY

20 THURSDAY

S	M	T	W	T	F	S
						1
2	3	4	5	6	7	8
9	10	11	12	13	14	15
16	17	18	19	20	21	22
23	24	25	26	27	28	29
30	31					

21 FRIDAY

22 SATURDAY

23 SUNDAY

HABIT TRACKER	M	T	W	T	F	S	S

What sparks joy?

MAY

24 MONDAY

25 TUESDAY

26 WEDNESDAY

27 THURSDAY

S	M	T	W	T	F	S
						1
2	3	4	5	6	7	8
9	10	11	12	13	14	15
16	17	18	19	20	21	22
23	24	25	26	27	28	29
30	31					

28 FRIDAY

29 SATURDAY

30 SUNDAY

HABIT TRACKER	M	T	W	T	F	S	S

What are you proud of?

MAY

S	M	T	W	T	F	S
						1
2	3	4	5	6	7	8
9	10	11	12	13	14	15
16	17	18	19	20	21	22
23	24	25	26	27	28	29
30	31					

31 MONDAY

1 TUESDAY

2 WEDNESDAY

3 THURSDAY

JUNE

S	M	T	W	T	F	S
		1	2	3	4	5
6	7	8	9	10	11	12
13	14	15	16	17	18	19
20	21	22	23	24	25	26
27	28	29	30			

4 FRIDAY

5 SATURDAY

6 SUNDAY

HABIT TRACKER	M	T	W	T	F	S	S

Free your creativity.

JUNE

7 MONDAY

8 TUESDAY

9 WEDNESDAY

10 THURSDAY

S	M	T	W	T	F	S
			1	2	3	4	5
6	7	8	9	10	11	12
13	14	15	16	17	18	19
20	21	22	23	24	25	26
27	28	29	30			

11 FRIDAY

12 SATURDAY

13 SUNDAY

HABIT TRACKER	M	T	W	T	F	S	S

Name a flower.

JUNE

14 MONDAY

15 TUESDAY

16 WEDNESDAY

17 THURSDAY

S	M	T	W	T	F	S
		1	2	3	4	5
6	7	8	9	10	11	12
13	14	15	16	17	18	19
20	21	22	23	24	25	26
27	28	29	30			

18 FRIDAY

19 SATURDAY

20 SUNDAY

HABIT TRACKER	M	T	W	T	F	S	S

Find the beauty in every day.

JUNE

21 MONDAY

22 TUESDAY

23 WEDNESDAY

24 THURSDAY

S	M	T	W	T	F	S
			1	2	3	4	5
6	7	8	9	10	11	12
13	14	15	16	17	18	19
20	21	22	23	24	25	26
27	28	29	30			

25 FRIDAY

26 SATURDAY

27 SUNDAY

HABIT TRACKER	M	T	W	T	F	S	S

What fills you with wonder?

JUNE

S	M	T	W	T	F	S
		1	2	3	4	5
6	7	8	9	10	11	12
13	14	15	16	17	18	19
20	21	22	23	24	25	26
27	28	29	30			

28 MONDAY

29 TUESDAY

30 WEDNESDAY

1 THURSDAY

JULY

S	M	T	W	T	F	S
				1	2	3
4	5	6	7	8	9	10
11	12	13	14	15	16	17
18	19	20	21	22	23	24
25	26	27	28	29	30	31

2 FRIDAY

3 SATURDAY

4 SUNDAY

HABIT TRACKER	M	T	W	T	F	S	S

Who has helped you on your journey?

JULY

5	MONDAY

6	TUESDAY

7	WEDNESDAY

8	THURSDAY

S	M	T	W	T	F	S
				1	2	3
4	5	6	7	8	9	10
11	12	13	14	15	16	17
18	19	20	21	22	23	24
25	26	27	28	29	30	31

9 FRIDAY

10 SATURDAY

11 SUNDAY

HABIT TRACKER	M	T	W	T	F	S	S

Create something just because.

JULY

12 MONDAY

13 TUESDAY

14 WEDNESDAY

15 THURSDAY

S	M	T	W	T	F	S
				1	2	3
4	5	6	7	8	9	10
11	12	13	14	15	16	17
18	19	20	21	22	23	24
25	26	27	28	29	30	31

16 FRIDAY

17 SATURDAY

18 SUNDAY

HABIT TRACKER	M	T	W	T	F	S	S

Treat yourself.

JULY

19 MONDAY

20 TUESDAY

21 WEDNESDAY

22 THURSDAY

S	M	T	W	T	F	S
				1	2	3
4	5	6	7	8	9	10
11	12	13	14	15	16	17
18	19	20	21	22	23	24
25	26	27	28	29	30	31

23 FRIDAY

24 SATURDAY

25 SUNDAY

HABIT TRACKER	M	T	W	T	F	S	S

Dance.

JULY

S	M	T	W	T	F	S
				1	2	3
4	5	6	7	8	9	10
11	12	13	14	15	16	17
18	19	20	21	22	23	24
25	26	27	28	29	30	31

26 MONDAY

27 TUESDAY

28 WEDNESDAY

29 THURSDAY

AUGUST

S M T W T F S
1 2 3 4 5 6 7
8 9 10 11 12 13 14
15 16 17 18 19 20 21
22 23 24 25 26 27 28
29 30 31

30 FRIDAY

31 SATURDAY

1 SUNDAY

HABIT TRACKER	M	T	W	T	F	S	S

What makes you happy?

AUGUST

2 MONDAY

3 TUESDAY

4 WEDNESDAY

5 THURSDAY

S	M	T	W	T	F	S
1	2	3	4	5	6	7
8	9	10	11	12	13	14
15	16	17	18	19	20	21
22	23	24	25	26	27	28
29	30	31				

6 FRIDAY

7 SATURDAY

8 SUNDAY

HABIT TRACKER	M	T	W	T	F	S	S

What have you created?

AUGUST

9 MONDAY

10 TUESDAY

11 WEDNESDAY

12 THURSDAY

S	M	T	W	T	F	S
	1	2	3	4	5	6	7
8	9	10	11	12	13	14
15	16	17	18	19	20	21
22	23	24	25	26	27	28
29	30	31				

13 FRIDAY

14 SATURDAY

15 SUNDAY

HABIT TRACKER	M	T	W	T	F	S	S

Imagine.

AUGUST

16 MONDAY

17 TUESDAY

18 WEDNESDAY

19 THURSDAY

S	M	T	W	T	F	S
1	2	3	4	5	6	7
8	9	10	11	12	13	14
15	16	17	18	19	20	21
22	23	24	25	26	27	28
29	30	31				

20 FRIDAY

21 SATURDAY

22 SUNDAY

HABIT TRACKER	M	T	W	T	F	S	S

Sing a song.

AUGUST

23 MONDAY

24 TUESDAY

25 WEDNESDAY

26 THURSDAY

S	M	T	W	T	F	S
1	2	3	4	5	6	7
8	9	10	11	12	13	14
15	16	17	18	19	20	21
22	23	24	25	26	27	28
29	30	31				

27 FRIDAY

28 SATURDAY

29 SUNDAY

HABIT TRACKER	M	T	W	T	F	S	S

Dive in.

AUGUST

S M T W T F S
1 2 3 4 5 6 7
8 9 10 11 12 13 14
15 16 17 18 19 20 21
22 23 24 25 26 27 28
29 30 31

30 MONDAY

31 TUESDAY

1 WEDNESDAY

2 THURSDAY

SEPTEMBER

S	M	T	W	T	F	S
				1	2	3	4
5	6	7	8	9	10	11
12	13	14	15	16	17	18
19	20	21	22	23	24	25
26	27	28	29	30		

3 FRIDAY

4 SATURDAY

5 SUNDAY

HABIT TRACKER	M	T	W	T	F	S	S

What positive habits would you like to adopt?

SEPTEMBER

6   MONDAY

7   TUESDAY

8   WEDNESDAY

9   THURSDAY

S	M	T	W	T	F	S
				1	2	3	4
5	6	7	8	9	10	11
12	13	14	15	16	17	18
19	20	21	22	23	24	25
26	27	28	29	30		

10 FRIDAY

11 SATURDAY

12 SUNDAY

HABIT TRACKER	M	T	W	T	F	S	S

What is your favorite color?

SEPTEMBER

13 MONDAY

14 TUESDAY

15 WEDNESDAY

16 THURSDAY

S	M	T	W	T	F	S
				1	2	3	4
5	6	7	8	9	10	11
12	13	14	15	16	17	18
19	20	21	22	23	24	25
26	27	28	29	30		

17 FRIDAY

18 SATURDAY

19 SUNDAY

HABIT TRACKER	M	T	W	T	F	S	S

Make your own magic.

SEPTEMBER

20 MONDAY

21 TUESDAY

22 WEDNESDAY

23 THURSDAY

S	M	T	W	T	F	S
				1	2	3	4
5	6	7	8	9	10	11
12	13	14	15	16	17	18
19	20	21	22	23	24	25
26	27	28	29	30

24 FRIDAY

25 SATURDAY

26 SUNDAY

HABIT TRACKER	M	T	W	T	F	S	S

Create.

SEPTEMBER

S	M	T	W	T	F	S
				1	2	3	4
5	6	7	8	9	10	11
12	13	14	15	16	17	18
19	20	21	22	23	24	25
26	27	28	29	30		

27 MONDAY

28 TUESDAY

29 WEDNESDAY

30 THURSDAY

OCTOBER

1 FRIDAY

2 SATURDAY

3 SUNDAY

HABIT TRACKER	M	T	W	T	F	S	S

Morning or night?

OCTOBER

4 MONDAY

5 TUESDAY

6 WEDNESDAY

7 THURSDAY

8 FRIDAY

9 SATURDAY

10 SUNDAY

HABIT TRACKER		M	T	W	T	F	S	S

What magic power would you like to have?

OCTOBER

11 MONDAY

12 TUESDAY

13 WEDNESDAY

14 THURSDAY

15 FRIDAY

16 SATURDAY

17 SUNDAY

HABIT TRACKER	M	T	W	T	F	S	S

Take a chance.

OCTOBER

18 MONDAY

19 TUESDAY

20 WEDNESDAY

21 THURSDAY

22 FRIDAY

23 SATURDAY

24 SUNDAY

HABIT TRACKER	M	T	W	T	F	S	S

Where would you love to go?

OCTOBER

25 MONDAY

26 TUESDAY

27 WEDNESDAY

28 THURSDAY

29 FRIDAY

30 SATURDAY

31 SUNDAY

HABIT TRACKER	M	T	W	T	F	S	S

Who do you want to be when you grow up?

NOVEMBER

1 MONDAY

2 TUESDAY

3 WEDNESDAY

4 THURSDAY

S	M	T	W	T	F	S
		1	2	3	4	5	6
7	8	9	10	11	12	13
14	15	16	17	18	19	20
21	22	23	24	25	26	27
28	29	30				

5 FRIDAY

6 SATURDAY

7 SUNDAY

HABIT TRACKER	M	T	W	T	F	S	S

What is your dream job?

NOVEMBER

8 MONDAY

9 TUESDAY

10 WEDNESDAY

11 THURSDAY

S	M	T	W	T	F	S
		1	2	3	4	5	6
7	8	9	10	11	12	13
14	15	16	17	18	19	20
21	22	23	24	25	26	27
28	29	30				

12 FRIDAY

13 SATURDAY

14 SUNDAY

HABIT TRACKER	M	T	W	T	F	S	S

Write a letter to yourself.

NOVEMBER

15 MONDAY

16 TUESDAY

17 WEDNESDAY

18 THURSDAY

S	M	T	W	T	F	S
		1	2	3	4	5	6
7	8	9	10	11	12	13
14	15	16	17	18	19	20
21	22	23	24	25	26	27
28	29	30				

19 FRIDAY

20 SATURDAY

21 SUNDAY

HABIT TRACKER	M	T	W	T	F	S	S

What do you want to create?

NOVEMBER

22 MONDAY

23 TUESDAY

24 WEDNESDAY

25 THURSDAY

S	M	T	W	T	F	S
		1	2	3	4	5	6
7	8	9	10	11	12	13
14	15	16	17	18	19	20
21	22	23	24	25	26	27
28	29	30				

26 FRIDAY

27 SATURDAY

28 SUNDAY

HABIT TRACKER	M	T	W	T	F	S	S

What are you amazing at?

NOVEMBER

S M T W T F S
1 2 3 4 5 6
7 8 9 10 11 12 13
14 15 16 17 18 19 20
21 22 23 24 25 26 27
28 29 30

29 MONDAY

30 TUESDAY

1 WEDNESDAY

2 THURSDAY

DECEMBER

S	M	T	W	T	F	S
				1	2	3	4
5	6	7	8	9	10	11
12	13	14	15	16	17	18
19	20	21	22	23	24	25
26	27	28	29	30	31	

3 FRIDAY

4 SATURDAY

5 SUNDAY

HABIT TRACKER	M	T	W	T	F	S	S

Make a wish.

DECEMBER

6 MONDAY

7 TUESDAY

8 WEDNESDAY

9 THURSDAY

S	M	T	W	T	F	S
				1	2	3	4
5	6	7	8	9	10	11
12	13	14	15	16	17	18
19	20	21	22	23	24	25
26	27	28	29	30	31	

10 FRIDAY

11 SATURDAY

12 SUNDAY

HABIT TRACKER	M	T	W	T	F	S	S

Where is your happy place?

DECEMBER

13 MONDAY

14 TUESDAY

15 WEDNESDAY

16 THURSDAY

S	M	T	W	T	F	S
			1	2	3	4
5	6	7	8	9	10	11
12	13	14	15	16	17	18
19	20	21	22	23	24	25
26	27	28	29	30	31	

17 FRIDAY

18 SATURDAY

19 SUNDAY

HABIT TRACKER	M	T	W	T	F	S	S

Follow your heart.

DECEMBER

20 MONDAY

21 TUESDAY

22 WEDNESDAY

23 THURSDAY

S	M	T	W	T	F	S
			1	2	3	4
5	6	7	8	9	10	11
12	13	14	15	16	17	18
19	20	21	22	23	24	25
26	27	28	29	30	31	

24 FRIDAY

25 SATURDAY

26 SUNDAY

HABIT TRACKER	M	T	W	T	F	S	S

No time like the present.

DECEMBER

S M T W T F S
1 2 3 4
5 6 7 8 9 10 11
12 13 14 15 16 17 18
19 20 21 22 23 24 25
26 27 28 29 30 31

27 MONDAY

28 TUESDAY

29 WEDNESDAY

30 THURSDAY

JANUARY

S	M	T	W	T	F	S
						1
2	3	4	5	6	7	8
9	10	11	12	13	14	15
16	17	18	19	20	21	22
23	24	25	26	27	28	29
30	31					

31 FRIDAY

1 SATURDAY

2 SUNDAY

HABIT TRACKER	M	T	W	T	F	S	S

Perfection doesn't exist.

Project _____

State Date _____ Deadline _____ Completed _____

Tasks

Resources

Notes

Project _____

State Date _____ Deadline _____ Completed _____

Tasks

Resources

Notes

Project _____

State Date _____ Deadline _____ Completed _____

Tasks

Resources

Notes

Project _____

State Date _____ Deadline _____ Completed _____

Tasks

Resources

Notes

Project _____

State Date _____ Deadline _____ Completed _____

Tasks

Resources

Notes

Project _____

State Date _____ Deadline _____ Completed _____

Tasks

Resources

Notes

Project _____

State Date _____ Deadline _____ Completed _____

Tasks

Resources

Notes

Project _____

State Date _____ Deadline _____ Completed _____

Tasks

Resources

Notes

Project _____

State Date _____ Deadline _____ Completed _____

Tasks

Resources

Notes

Project _____

State Date _____ Deadline _____ Completed _____

Tasks

Resources

Notes

Project _____

State Date _____ Deadline _____ Completed _____

Tasks

Resources

Notes

Project _____

State Date _____ Deadline _____ Completed _____

Tasks

Resources

Notes